National museum Message Biblique Marc Chagall

National museum Message Biblique Marc Chagall

Jean-Michel Foray
Curator, national museum Message Biblique Marc Chagall

Françoise Rossini-Paquet
Researcher, national museum Message Biblique Marc Chagall

Réunion
des Musées
Nationaux

National museum Message Biblique Marc Chagall
Avenue du Docteur Ménard, 06000 Nice

ISBN: 2-7118-3938-9

© Editions de la Réunion des musées nationaux
49, rue Etienne-Marcel, 75001 Paris. 2000
© A.D.A.G.P. 2000

"The Bible has captured my imagination ever since I was a very young child. To me, it has always seemed the greatest source of poetry the world has ever known. Since then, I have sought its reflection in life and in art. The Bible is like a resonance of nature, and that secret is what I have tried to transmit."

Marc Chagall

Contents

National museum Message Biblique Marc Chagall

In 1966, Marc Chagall donated the paintings that today form the core of the collection of the Musée National Message Biblique in Nice to the French government. This considerable body of work includes: a series of seventeen large, monumental paintings illustrating the first two books of the Bible – Genesis and Exodus – and the Song of Songs; thirty-nine gouaches painted in 1931 and 1932 as preparatory sketches for the Bible illustrations, which the art dealer Ambroise Vollard had commissioned him to do; etchings; and lithographs. It is a very particular group because it is entirely devoted to Biblical themes, which are central to Chagall's work as a whole. Although the artist dealt with other topics, the Bible remained central to his preoccupations and recurred often, forming a running thread through his work. The decision to donate this group to the French government was therefore an important choice. Chagall did not want to create a museum showing works that were painted about various themes and during different periods. Rather, his goal was to bequeath a sort of aesthetic manifesto and a spiritual message. For Chagall did not share his contemporaries' artistic concepts. For him, art is basically religious in the etymological sense of the word: it is a connection, a link, and the Bible, which twentieth-century artists completely ignored, remains "the greatest source of poetry the world has ever known" and "the world's greatest work of art". Illustrating, or, more exactly, commenting on the Bible was a way of providing art with meaning and a social function at the same time.

When the Musée National Message Biblique was inaugurated, Chagall said, "If every life inevitably moves towards its end, we must, during our own, color it with the colors of love and hope. The social logic of life and the

Marc Chagall

in his New York

studio

1942

essence of every religion is in this love. For me, perfection in Art and in life flows from the Biblical spring. Without that spirit, the mechanics of logic and construction alone, in Art as in life, will not bear fruit."

In his very singular relationship to the Bible, Chagall was very different from the great twentieth-century artists who were his contemporaries. Some of them – Matissse, for example – may have decorated a chapel or designed sacerdotal vestments, but always for a specific commission. Others, such as Léger, especially during the post-war reconstruction of France, designed stained-glass windows for destroyed churches that had been rebuilt. None except Chagall, however, tackled Biblical themes headlong and so consistently responded to religious commissions. His personal feelings about the Bible – "the Bible has captured my imagination ever since I was a very young child", he said – determined his position as an artist: "I chose painting; to me, it seemed as indispensable as food. It seemed to me to be a window through which I could fly away into another world. In that regard, pardon me for recalling the Biblical image of a stuttering Moses, but whom God pursued so that he would fulfill his duty. Thus, all of us – despite our stuttering – somebody is pursuing all of us to do our duty[1]."

And if being an artist is a duty, the obvious implication is that art has a social function. During his inaugural speech for the museum, Chagall said, "Perhaps young and not-so-young people searching for an ideal of brotherhood and love, such as my colors and lines have dreamed it, will come into this house."

The social function of art – uniting men and women in a communion of thought and feelings – finds its fulfillment in a special place which, despite the Biblical theme, is not a house of worship. That is what Chagall was probably thinking of when he said in 1963, "I think I will continue the Bible series I have started, intended later for a building that will be neither a chapel, nor a museum, but a place where all those who are seeking a new spiritual and plastic content (of the work of art) about which I have spoken will feel welcome[2]."

At first, the twelve paintings that illustrate Genesis and Exodus were designed for the Calvary chapel in Vence, where Chagall had thought of displaying them when he began working on the Biblical Message. Indeed, a Calvary chapel with a sacristy and small, spaced-out votive chapels dedicated to the Stations of the Cross were located close to his studio in Vence. All these buildings had been disaffected for several years, and some Vence municipal council members had thought of asking Chagall to decorate them. The artist eagerly accepted their offer, which is demonstrated by the many preparatory studies he made at that time. The twelve Biblical Message paintings were originally to decorate the twelve walls of the Calvary chapel, whose floor plan is in the shape of a Latin cross, and the five Song of Songs paintings were to be placed in the adjoining sacristy. Chagall took the chapel's dimensions into account, which explains why the paintings are of different sizes. However, humidity was seeping into the chapel's stones, and for purposes of conservation Chagall had to give up on the idea of displaying his paintings there.

1. Lecture given at the University of Chicago, 1968. Museum archives.
2. Symposium held in Washington, DC in 1962. Published in *Bridges of Human Understanding*, University Publisher, New York, 1964.

The museum

But the paintings were finished. Chagall gave them to the French government, which accepted the donation and turned them into the core of the museum's collection. André Malraux, the minister of culture under Charles De Gaulle, established the Chagall museum as a national museum, and as such it was natural to locate it in Paris. But the museum moved to Nice as part of the decentralization policy under way. Chagall wanted it to be located in a peaceful place: the Olivetto plot on the Cimiez hill was chosen because it was an olive grove, of which several trees have been preserved in the garden, given by the City of Nice to the French government in 1968.

Chagall thus became the first living artist in France to have a museum designed and built to house his work. Right from the start, he was able to cooperate with the architect appointed by the director of French museums, André Hermant (1908-1978), and organize with him the design and layout of the exhibition spaces.

André Hermant was an avowed disciple of Auguste Perret's – in other words, a modernist who was preoccupied with questions of functionalism. Nevertheless, he managed to give all his buildings a personal touch: in any case, the Chagall museum is a model of architecture that has been specially

designed for works of art, and the building teaches us that adapting structures to art works does not necessarily mean that they lose their identity. The Chagall museum, which so admirably does the artist honor, features a powerful, original design. Chagall and Hermant worked together and probably drew up many versions before settling on the final project. The evidence for this assumption lies in the fact that they drafted a succession of plans between 1963 and 1968, when construction on the final project got under way. In fact, the architect had designed the museum's basic structure very early on. It was built like a huge villa overhanging the city of Nice, with the entrance facing the hill and the façade facing the sea. Visitors walk through a dark porch before entering a spacious hall resembling the nave of a church, where the Message Biblique is on display, illuminated by natural light. This is the only room in the museum with a solemn character: the high ceiling and vast space confer a sense of monumentality on the paintings. The lateral lighting fosters the impression of being in a home rather than museum. With its simple floor plan – two orthogonal bars, one for the Biblical Message, the other for all the remaining rooms and the service areas – lateral lighting and hillside location, the building Hermant designed successfully blends religious symbolism (the contrasts between darkness and light, the stained-glass windows of the auditorium) with a sense of intimacy (the pool, the terrace and glimpses of the surrounding countryside). The paintings in the main hall, which were hung in the way that Chagall himself wanted them to be, do not follow in chronological order: visitors are guided more by the artist's sensibility than by an imposed itinerary[3].

The Biblical Message

Chagall was born in 1887 in Lyozno, a town near the small city of Vitebsk in present-day Belarus, where his family moved shortly afterwards. He was brought up in a religiously-observant Jewish household where the Bible was read out loud and the year was punctuated by the cycle of religious holidays. Chagall left Vitebsk for Saint Petersburg in 1907. From there he went to Paris in 1910, returning to Vitebsk in 1914, which he left for Moscow in 1920 before moving back to Paris four years later.

One thing is sure: travel and exile never led Chagall far from Vitebsk and its churches, synagogues and the Jewish world he observed with tenderness, humor and irony, as many of the drawings from the Russian years demonstrate. But Chagall was an astute observer of the Christian world as well. In paintings from the Russian period, there is always at least one church for each synagogue, one Orthodox procession for every Jewish wedding. That world features regularly in Chagall's work, even in the late paintings he made in Vence during the 1960s. For example, Vence is depicted in the third painting from the Song of Song series, but, like a reflection in a lake, Vitebsk appears with an onion-domed Russian Orthodox church and wooden houses.

Chagall never really got over leaving Russia. Unlike other, slightly younger Jewish artists from the same, vast area around the Baltic Sea who settled in the

3. On André Hermant, see Nathalie Roulleau, *André Hermant, architecte et urbaniste (1908-1978)*, Ph.D. thesis, University of Aix-Marseilles I, 1998.

*The main hall
of the museum*

United States – the names of Mark Rothko and Barnett Newman most readily spring to mind – Chagall always remained a Russian. The two Americans, whose works were emblematic of abstract modernism, probably experienced a little homesickness late in life. In 1956, Newman painted a fourteen-part work called *The Stations of the Cross* subtitled *Lama Sabachatani,* the last words, in Russian, that Christ uttered before dying. In 1960, Rothko began decorating the chapel of Saint Patrick's University in Houston (later, in 1972, after the artist's death, the chapel became an ecumenical house of worship). During the same period, Chagall started painting the *Biblical Message,* but that series formed a continuum with his previous work.

Biblical themes in Chagall's work were nothing new. They appeared as early as 1912 in *Madonna with Child* and *The Holy Family.* They featured in the gouaches painted during the 1930s and the etchings commissioned by Vollard to illustrate the Bible. Afterwards, Chagall dealt with religious themes on a regular basis, focusing especially on the Crucifixion in the 1940s and 1950s. They were from the New Testament, but others attest to the life-long persistence of his interest in rites (for example, he often painted depictions of marriage ceremonies and wedding engagements) and to houses of worship (synagogues and churches).

Chagall had a religious upbringing, and the Vitebsk area was home to a particular Jewish tradition. Hassidism, which was popular among impoverished Jews, is based on a spontaneous relationship with God, the profound unity of the world and God's presence everywhere and in everything. Hassidic Jews do not believe that the world is divided into distinct, separate entities, but united in an active interaction between all things. Everything holds together. That is taught by Hassidism as well as by the Kabala from which it is derived, and the Zohar, a basic work of Jewish mysticism: God, the soul and the universe do not lead separate lives, each on a different plane. Their division is the cosmic consequence of Man's sin, but in the original act of creation they formed a colorful whole made up of three closely-related parts. It took no effort for Chagall, who had a religious spirit and observed the world with a sense of wonderment, to spontaneously see beings and things swept along in perpetual motion where there is neither top nor bottom, where the natural and the supernatural mingle and where love and spiritual feeling are two sides of the same coin.

From the beginning, Chagall did not think of his painting as activity cut off from the rest of the world or belonging to landscape or portrait genres alone. That is why, as early as 1912 – and this may be what immediately characterizes his work the best—he painted total descriptions, not rejecting anything around him. For example, especially in the 1910s and 1920s, a man discreetly urinating against a wooden stockade fence, or a sensuous nude, might be seen in the lower right-hand corner of a painting featuring Vitebsk. Other works show animals, objects, street scenes, snippets of community life, figures of the artist's father, uncles or friends and his love for his fiancée Bella, with whom he portrayed himself floating in the air above the city, literally carried away with happiness. The religious scenes naturally feature in these depictions of the painter's entourage; they are at home in this pictorial world, they belong there: the Madonna with child alongside the cattle dealer.

The *Biblical Message*, then, is closely related to all the artist's work that came before it. It is not one theme among others, but the continuation of a lifelong preoccupation with religion, which, as is often the case with this painter, often refers to something other than religion itself.

Chagall's artistic vocabulary is eminently metaphorical: words are taken literally. The artist takes the drunken man who is said to have lost his mind, and paints a drinker who sees his head next to his body. He who is free as the wind floats in the air, he who is happy as a fish in water swims in the sea. In his paintings, words constantly refer to images and vice versa. Whimsical, often humorous hybrid monsters, giants, flying rabbis, musical fish and clock-birds offer us a view and a description of the world revealing the values

Vitebsk, at the end of the 19th century

Chagall with his wife and his daughter, Ida

1917

Chagall cared about, the milestones around which our lives are built: love, passing time, flowers as a symbol of pleasure. On a more serious note, religious scenes evoke human history: wars, displacements of populations, exoduses. The crowds in some of the religious works from the 1940s easily bring to mind the tragedy of World War Two.

If Chagall depicted the world around him, in all its humblest and simplest aspects, it was natural for him to also become a history painter when events took an obviously historical turn. The works from the 1950s displayed at the museum (*Triptych*), and which follow the works he painted during the war years, also have an epic dimension. Village life, Paris seen through the artist's window and *Lovers on their Cloud* are not all that Chagall is describing; he is also depicting the life of a people, the great moments in its history and the turning points in its destiny. It is striking to see how different the Bible illustrations commissioned by Vollard in the 1930s are from the large paintings in the Biblical Message series. Crowds are scarce, but the characters Chagall liked so much – Noah, Moses and Abraham – are depicted at the most crucial moments of their stories: Abraham about to sacrifice his son, Moses receiving the Tables of the Law. There are no witnesses to these acts in the paintings, setting up a direct relationship between us, the onlookers, and them.

Later – and probably because Chagall had gone through, as he put it, "the tragedy of the life in and around us, along with everybody else living through this age" – the same scenes are populated with witnesses. In the 1931 gouache *The Rainbow, Sign of the Covenant between God and the Earth*, illustrating a chapter from Genesis, Noah is alone with an angel, just as Abraham was alone

*The Rainbow, Sign
of the Covenant
between God and
the Earth*
1931
Gouache
H. 63,5 ; L. 47,5 cm

in another gouache from the same series, *Abraham Ready to Immolate His Son*. In paintings on the same theme dating from between 1960 and 1966, other people are in the scene. The portrayals of Noah, the angel and the rainbow stand out against a complex background teeming with a crowd running away from a burning village and a smattering of characters, including King David, Moses, Christ, figures that are half-man, half-beast, symbolic scenes, Adam and Eve in the garden of Eden, a lamb and a family that recalls the many depictions of the Holy Family in classical art. The background is a mixed, colorful world where figures of violence and of happiness rub shoulders, and where figures from the imagination (the man with the head of an ass, the flying fish) are beside others taken from real life. In Genesis, Noah had a vision of the rainbow in his sleep: thus, Chagall mixes figures from the dream with figures from the exodus and from the dream of life. Similarly, in *The Sacrifice of Isaac*, history is summoned up by the portrayal of Christ carrying the cross, by a character symbolizing Vitebsk and by a mother and child.

*Abraham ready to
Immolate his Son*
1931
Oil and gouache
H. 62 ; L. 48,5 cm

From the gouaches of the 1930s to the paintings of the 1960s, history pervaded Chagall's work. The rather serious tone of the works in the Biblical Message has less to do with their topics than with the background against which the figures stand out and which forms a sort of commentary on the Biblical episode that each painting illustrates. By creating a cycle of works, Chagall carries on an artistic tradition of illustrating scenes from the Old Testament. Rembrandt and Veronese painted Abraham about to sacrifice Isaac; the Dutch master and Delacroix made paintings of Jacob struggling with the angel. But he also fits in with a specifically Jewish tradition: the Talmudic tradition of commentary. In Judaism, the Torah – the first five books of the Bible – is the word of God. It is therefore not intelligible or representable on its own. The Talmud, the set of commentaries on the sacred text, is required to understand it.

Sylvie Forestier[4] suggested that Chagall wanted to add his own commentary of the Torah. That would be the meaning of the Biblical Message: like the commentaries, it makes the word of God intelligible.

On a more down-to-earth note, the museum's thousands of visitors, who are certainly not all familiar with the Western, Judeo-Christian tradition, are attracted by the peace and harmony they find there. Chagall's faith in Man and in love can be felt in the rooms, thanks to the successful marriage between the paintings and the architecture.

The paintings are at home here. And visitors discover the qualities that have made Chagall's works so popular: the incredible chromatic richness, the wise combination of colors. And they also discover that, before venturing metaphysical or religious interpretations of the paintings, it is first necessary to consider them the fruit of work. Similarly to Rothko, who was mentioned above, and whose oeuvre has also been interpreted from a religious point of view, Chagall's painstaking work on color – the very medium of painting – is what gives the paintings all their power. With Chagall, color is so subtle that it can give rise to endless interpretations. Those interpretations, the discourse that we, the viewers, add to the works, are sketched out by the painting's topic, but the colors are so strong and powerful that they leave the way for interpretation open, free and, especially, possible for all those who – and there are many of them among our visitors – know nothing of Abraham, Noah and Moses. So it is not so much what the artist wanted us to know, whether Biblical or profane, which makes them work, as the ability that he gave them to be open to several emotions and ideas. In that respect, Chagall, who often painted flowers, made his work what they are: a universal source of pleasure.

Chagall in
his studio,
August 1934

4. Sylvie Forestier, *Les Chagall de Chagall*, Paris, Albin Michel, 1988.

Genesis and Exodus

Twelve of the 17 large *Biblical Message* paintings focus on Genesis and Exodus. This group is a cycle about the history of a people. The five remaining paintings depict the Song of Songs, which form a homogenous series on love.

The works in the *Biblical Message* are still hanging the way the artist intended them to – not in the chronological order of the Bible story but as a group composition. Visitors, their eyes drawn by a dominant color or subject, may stroll from one work to the next.

Marc Chagall
in Vence
1980

The Creation of Man

1956-1958

Oil on canvas

H. 299; L. 200.5 cm.

Two different accounts of the Creation introduce Genesis. Chagall chose to illustrate the second, which mentions the Garden of Eden.

The work's theme is the initial creation and development of man. It is animated by a descending angel with spread-out wings carrying a completely languid Adam: God has not yet given him the breath of life. The angel's arm merges with the rest of Adam's body. The angel, an ephebe, turns his head away from the man he is poised to lay down in the Garden of Eden. The celestial creature is wearing a pair of trousers, perhaps to look more human.

The diagonal line running from the angel's body to the painting's upper left-hand corner is crowned by a ball of fire, a fantastic sun with rainbow-colored rays that recall the bond between God and man, and the future covenant that He will seal with the Jewish people.

The Bible story figures revolve in the sun's spiraling rays. The hunched-over prophet Jeremiah is lamenting the loss of Jerusalem. A man – perhaps Aaron – carrying a *menorah*[1], whose seven branches symbolize the seven days of the Creation, points out Jacob's ladder. A rabbi with a goat's head carries the Torah scroll, while King David, of whom Chagall was particularly fond, plays his harp amidst the Jewish people. The village built of wooden boards is Vitebsk, where Chagall was born. Christ is shown with the *tallith*[2], the Jewish prayer shawl, wrapped around his hips.

The hands of God emerge from the sky holding the Tables of the Law out to a small, winged Moses with a green face, while an angel blows into a *shofar*[3]. Above the ball of fire, an angel with four wings holds out a flower offering, like a cherub guarding the Ark.

Yellow, the celestial light, and the red of human passions respond to blue, symbol of the Garden of Eden's calm and serenity.

In the bottom right-hand corner of the painting, a tender couple and animals still in peace evoke the atmosphere of Eden before the Fall.

1. *Menorah:* seven-branched candelabrum.
2. *Thallit* (or *talit* or *shallit*): prayer shawl.
3. *Shofar:* ram's horn ritual instrument.

Paradise

1961

Oil on canvas

H. 198; L. 288 cm.

This Garden of Eden, a mixture of green and blue tones with touches of yellow and red, is a tribute to nature. Bouquets of flowers, angels and chimerical animals surround Adam and Eve, who hold each other in a tight embrace. Adam's leg merges with Eve's. Chagall experienced the kind of love in which two souls seem to fuse into one, first with Bella, then with Valentina.

The original couple is depicted twice: during the creation of Eve and when the pair become one flesh.

On the left-hand side, Adam is shown in a yoga pose, with one arm lifted, revealing the flank from which God removed the rib to create Eve, who seems to be floating above his head. Imaginary animals and other-worldly creatures – feathered fishes and birds of paradise with elaborate plumage – are revolving around this scene. The first man and woman are living in harmony with beasts. Eve is listening to the faun-headed Lucifer.

In another part of the painting, the coiled, tempting serpent and a bouquet symbolizing the Tree of Life are next to Adam, who is covering up his and Eve's nakedness.

Adam and Eve being driven out of Paradise

1961

Oil on canvas

H. 190; L. 283.5 cm.

Chagall did not paint the story of the Fall but of a Loss: the loss of the Garden of Eden. Everything is upside-down in this painting, which has neither top nor bottom. There are flying fish, goat-headed roosters and trees growing upside-down. An absolutely luminous bouquet – a rare warm touch in a range of green tones – recalls Moses's burning bush. In the fireworks bouquet, the flowers' stems are not shown, merely suggested. A white light symbolizing the word of God floats above the bouquet. A sword-wielding archangel is chasing Adam and Eve, who are not sad. They are taking a red rooster with them, the symbol of life and hope.

The first couple disobeyed the word of God. Driven out of Paradise where they lived in harmony with His other creatures, they are now aware of free will. This painting seems to suggest that rules were meant to be broken. Paradise was a dream and the tempting serpent is a witness to their exile. Above them, on the opposite bank of the river of Paradise, Chagall depicted himself painting: the artist becomes the interface between God and humanity. First, people had angels as messengers; now, they have artists, and Chagall often showed himself as an angel. Near the easel, a small, violet-colored woman with an upside-down head poetically symbolizes the Fall.

Noah's Ark

1961-1966

Oil on canvas

H. 236; L. 234 cm.

Compared with most classic depictions, Chagall painted his Noah's Ark from a surprising viewpoint: the interior. A crowd squeezes in around the window from which Noah releases the dove; people and animals mingle in an elliptical movement. A few spots of color – Noah's green face, a woman's pink arm, a doe's yellow pelage, a peacock's multi-colored plumage – add warmth to this watery world.

Noah's family crowds together on the right-hand side of the painting. There is a heart-warming image of a mother protecting her child, wrapping him in her arms.

The figures have peaceful expressions on their faces. They are safe and sound.

On the left, Jacob's ladder, which appears in many of Chagall's paintings, is a gateway to heaven. The window from which Noah releases the dove that will return carrying an olive branch represents another choice: the profane.

In the painting's upper left-hand corner, Chagall did a self-portrait of himself witnessing the scene.

Noah and the Rainbow

1961-1966

Oil on canvas

H. 205; L. 292.5 cm.

The symbol of the covenant between God and the Jewish people is a rainbow that Chagall painted completely white. A bearded angel shows Noah this heavenly sign. Chagall illustrates the sign of God's intervention with an angel, a bearded man recalling the traditional Christian depiction of God. All the colors of the rainbow are distributed around the canvas like touches of the colors of hope.

Noah is lying down (in Hebrew, his name means "he who rests"), his head reposing on his hand. He almost looks like a blue mandorla, bathing in the serenity resulting from communion with the word of God.

A calf that the patriarch will slaughter and burn on the altar as an offering lies upside-down at his feet. This sacrifice echoes the flames burning the house in the center of the painting.

Near the house, a panicked, tearful crowd of people is fleeing. Like a bridge between two epochs, the holocaust Noah offers after coming out of the Ark is echoed by twentieth-century pogroms.

This work features a symmetry of extremes. Adam and Eve, King David, flying figures and naked women on the right-hand side of the painting seem to symbolize the serenity and immeasurable happiness of the covenant with God. On the left, Icarus with the head of a goat, Moses, flying figures with dislocated bodies and a even a bride fall into an abyss of fear, hopelessness, war and persecution.

The hope embodied by Noah contrasts with the despair of the Chosen People, who seem to be paying the price for breaking God's laws.

Abraham and the three Angels

1960-1966

Oil on canvas

H. 190; L. 292 cm.

The painting of Abraham and the three angels in the main room is the only work featuring red as the dominant color. The influence of the icons in Moscow's Tretriakov gallery was not lost on Chagall, who must have seen them. The artist was steeped in Russian Orthodox culture. The deep red tones and the golden wings recall the colors of the icons.

The visit of the three angels to Abraham is a classic theme of Russian icons. They have come to make two announcements: the future motherhood of Sarah, who had been barren until then, and the destruction of Sodom and Gomorrah. They are shown before a feast.

In traditional icons, the angels gaze at the viewer, but in this work Chagall has them sitting on a bench with their backs turned to us. The angels seem to be pushed towards the viewer by an optical effect due to a "cubist" representation of luminous rays.

Abraham and Sarah are standing near their guests, the patriarch adopting a deeply respectful attitude. His hands are turned towards his chest as a sign of acceptance of the divine message. In the background behind them, the couple's open house symbolizes their hospitality.

The angels' downy, spread-out wings seem to be coming out of the painting.

In the upper right-hand corner, Abraham is accompanying the angels on the road to Sodom and Gomorrah inside a bubble similar to that of a comic strip.

Abraham sacrificing Issac

1960-1966

Oil on canvas

H. 230.5; L. 235 cm.

God wanted to test Abraham by asking him to kill his own son, the most abominable deed that any man could perform. The patriarch asked Issac to gather wood for the sacrifice and went to place indicated by God. Artists from every period have depicted this biblical episode many times. In this work, Chagall takes up Rembrandt's composition in the painting at Saint Petersburg's Hermitage museum.

Abraham lays his son down on the pile of wood. He is holding a knife, his face bathed in a red that is the color of blood. His son's body, diffused with light, is offered up to God. The brown tones in the upper right-hand corner of the painting respond to the brown tones of the wood on which Issac is lying. The child's martyrdom echoes the martyrdom of the Jewish people in flight, the martyrdom of Christ and the martyrdom of exile.

A luminous white angel sends a blue angel with an arching body to stop Abraham in the nick of time. A diagonal line between the two angels and Abraham symbolizes the bond between God and man. Behind a tree, Sarah, both hands upturned towards her face, is desperate. The ram that will take Issac's place is near her.

Jacob's Dream

1960-1966

Oil on canvas

H. 230.5; L. 235 cm.

This painting cannot be dissociated from *Jacob Wrestling with the Angel.* Both works feature the same blue and purple tones, setting the scene at night.

Jacob's Dream is a diptych. The dominant blue and mauve tones whisk us into a prophetic, poetic world of dreams.

The sleeping Jacob is in the purple part of the painting, as if he were in deepest night. He seems to be admiring the angels, who, like acrobats, hold the seven-step ladder – seven, as in the number of days that it took for God to create the world. An angel of light is standing atop the ladder, while another angel blows into a *shofar.*

In the upper right-hand corner of the painting, a cherub with four spread-out wings is hovering in blue space. He is holding a *menorah,* a symbol of divine light, with six instead of the traditional seven branches.

Abraham sacrificing Issac is in the lower-right hand corner. This illustration underscores the covenant between God and Abraham and, by extension, between God and the children of Abraham. A depiction of Christ on the cross appears in the painting's upper part. A diagonal line between the crucified son of God's head, the cherub's head and Jacob's head seems to connect the work's two main scenes.

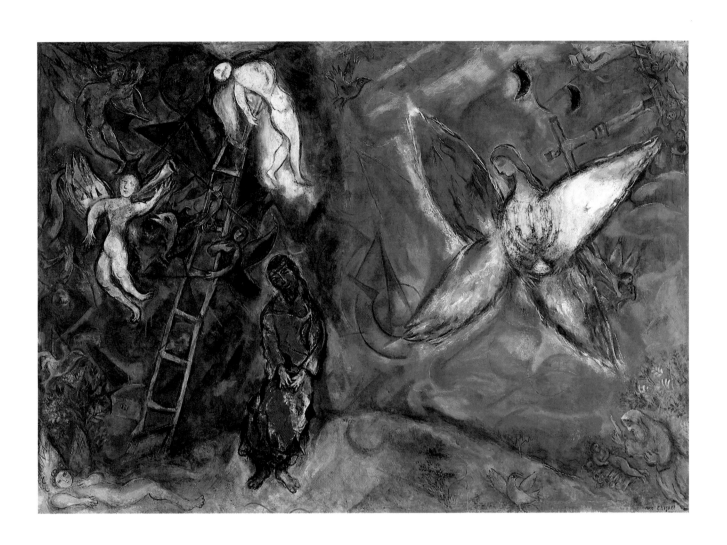

Jacob wrestling with the Angel

1960-1966

Oil on canvas

H. 251; L. 205 cm.

Chagall depicted this Old Testament story like a dream. The deep blue tones indicate that the struggle took place in the middle of the night. The angel is an other-worldly creature: his leafy feathers seem to give his wings movement. He is much larger than Jacob, and his right hand is on his opponent's forehead, as if to bless him. This is the end of the struggle.

The combat takes place in the air above a village that can be identified as Vitebsk because of the wooden boards.

As is often the case in Chagall's works, the main scene of the struggle is surrounded by other episodes. Like the narrative icons that the artist saw in Russian Orthodox churches, the story of Jacob is told in two secondary scenes on either side of the wrestlers.

A married couple united in an embrace appears in the upper left-hand corner of the painting. They can be identified as Jacob and Rachel because of the well in the background. Jacob and Rachel met at a well, a vital place in the nomadic, desert society to which they belonged.

Symmetrical to this scene, Chagall depicted an episode that occurred after Jacob's struggle with the angel (his marriage to Rachel took place before): the story of Joseph, one of twelve sons begotten by four different wives. Rachel – his favorite – gave birth to Joseph and Benjamin. Joseph was the apple of Jacob's eye, and out of jealousy his brothers stripped him naked and threw him into a well.

But above this scene Chagall painted a golden rooster, the symbol of hope and a herald of the dawn. Indeed, Joseph did not perish in the well.

Lastly, in the lower right-hand corner Jeremiah is hunched over a white piece of cloth and lamenting the loss of Jerusalem, a disaster in the history of the Jewish people, which occurred later.

In this painting, Chagall connected the story of Jeremiah, a single man, with the history of the entire Jewish people. Indeed, Jacob was the father of the twelve tribes of Israel.

Moses before the Burning Bush

1960-1966

Oil on canvas

H. 195; L. 312 cm.

The three last paintings in the *Biblical Message* series depict episodes from Exodus. *Moses Before the Burning Bush* is a diptych. But unlike *Jacob's Dream*, Chagall chose to illustrate two scenes from the life of Moses. From right to left, the artist painted his quiet life in the pastures of Madian. On the side is his brother Aaron, who was of great help to him and never left his side. The patriarch has a beatific expression on his face as he gazes at the burning bush. Chagall always identified Moses with rays, the illustration of the light that his face radiated when he came back down from the top of Mount Sinai with the Ten Commandments.

The burning bush is in the middle of the painting. Above, an angel, a messenger from God, appears in a circle. The colors of the fiery bush can also be seen in the angel's double halo: they are the colors of the rainbow. Once again, Chagall recalls the dialogue and the covenant between God and man.

On the left side of the painting, the Hebrews can be seen leaving Egypt and crossing the Red Sea. The high, yellow head of Moses is turned towards an area outside the bounds of the painting. The Tables of the Law, which he has not yet received but which already confer his total authority over the Hebrews, are in front of him. His mantle is the Jewish people; they are his flesh. In the lower part of the mantle, a wave swallows up Pharaoh's army. The bodies are dislocated. The serenity of the Hebrews marching towards freedom stands in sharp contrast with the dramatic fate of the Egyptian army.

Moses striking the Rock

1960-1966

Oil on canvas

H. 237; L. 232 cm.

This brown-toned painting contrasts with the bright palette of the *Biblical Message* as a whole. Chagall chose a non-geometrical composition in order to symbolize the wandering of the Jewish people in the desert. The tightly-packed crowd overruns the painting, only the curving line of the water's flow separating it into two groups. The people are confident; they are holding recipients to fill with water. Moses strikes the rock with his stick and the water gushes forth, quenching the thirst of people and livestock alike.

Moses has received the Tables of the Law. He is empowered with authority over the Jewish people and there, in the desert, in accordance with the word of God, he strikes the rock of Horeb to make the water flow. Chagall wanted to seize that moment and, without taking forms into consideration, scattered luminous spots of green, yellow, red, violet and blue – the colors of the rainbow – around the painting.

Moses receiving the Tables of the Law

1960-1966

Oil on canvas

H. 237; L. 233 cm.

This painting, which is near the Creation, completes the cycle. Chagall's illustration of Moses receiving the Tables of the Law closes the direct dialogue with God. From now on, messengers and prophets will be the intermediaries between Him and man.

This yellow-toned painting is bathed in divine light and structured by two criss-crossing diagonal lines.

One diagonal line symbolizes the bond between Moses and God. The patriarch is standing on a rock, but at the same time he is carried by his people, waiting at the bottom of Mount Sinai. Running out of patience, they break the word of God given to Moses. The despairing Hebrews fashion a golden calf, an idol to replace the abstract God of Moses, a concept that they fail to understand.

Chagall does not show the face of God, but he painted His hands coming out of gray clouds. God holds the Tables of the Law out to Moses, whose body stretches towards heaven.

The other diagonal line is formed by mountains reaching up to the sky. At the bottom, the figure carrying the *menorah* is Aaron, Moses's brother. On his chest, he is wearing the breastplate of a Hebrew high priest, with twelve precious stones representing the twelve tribes of Israel.

Above Aaron, the presence of Jeremiah and David recalls various breaches of the covenant between man and God. Jeremiah announces the fall of Jerusalem because the Chosen People had not followed God's rules. King David coveted the wife of another man, whom he had killed. God took the life of the illegitimate son he had with Bathsheba to punish him. The misdeeds of the people echo the sins of David, on the two sides of the painting.

The Song of Songs

Five paintings dedicated to "Vava, my joy and my happiness" are on display in this hexagonal room, which is shaped like the heart of a Star of David. Unlike the room with the paintings of the *Biblical Message*, this place is dedicated to love: There is no mention of God in the Song of Songs, also known as the Song of Solomon or the Canticle of Canticles. The colors are also different. Blue and green tones dominate the main room, while pink and red are the most prominent colors here.

The Song of Songs celebrates the love between a man and woman who meet, separate, look for each other and reunite. The man may be Solomon, the peaceful king, and the woman the Sulamite, the pacified. The Sulamite has been compared to the Sunamite, who appeared in the story of David and of Solomon. And the authorship of the Song of Song is attributed to Solomon.

But this room also celebrates the love of David and Bathsheba.

The Song of Songs I

1960

Oil on paper mounted

on canvas

H. 146.5; L. 171.5 cm.

The couple in the foreground is entwined in a strange embrace. The woman has the body of a rooster with deep red, incandescent feathers, and her head is resting on the man's chest. A dove hovers over their embrace. A diagonal line leads to another couple, who are clearly identified as a king and his beloved. They seem poised to take flight. Love of music and nature are very clearly suggested. A bird strums a lyre, and a little musician plays a flute in the middle of a flowering bush.

The throne of Jerusalem and the Star of David are in the upper right-hand corner. An open book – perhaps the Song of Songs – is in the lower left-hand corner diagonally across from them. In the painting's right-hand margin, the outline of a naked woman stands out against a deep-red city shrouded in darkness. This scene seems to illustrate the dream described in the Song of Songs in which the woman searches for her beloved in the streets of Jerusalem at night.

The Song of Songs II

1960

Oil on paper mounted

on canvas

H. 139; L. 164 cm.

A woman lying languidly in a blossoming bush seems to be asleep, dreaming. The slumbering figure's nakedness evokes the verse, "By night on my bed I sought him whom my soul loveth." It is also possible that this woman offering herself and lying on the Tree of Life is Bella. The Tree of Life is lying down, Bella is no more, but another woman is seated at the bottom of the tree: Valentina, who is also the beloved.

Both women are the object of the same love. The abandoned body's very pale color gives the painting a voluptuous atmosphere.

A hand above Jerusalem is stretching out towards the moon, a symbol of womanhood.

On either side of the tree, a winged King David accompanies this woman on her journey to the world of dreams on his lyre. Near him and Solomon's throne, and beneath the tree, the city of Jerusalem, can be identified by the Tower of David and the Dome of the Rock.

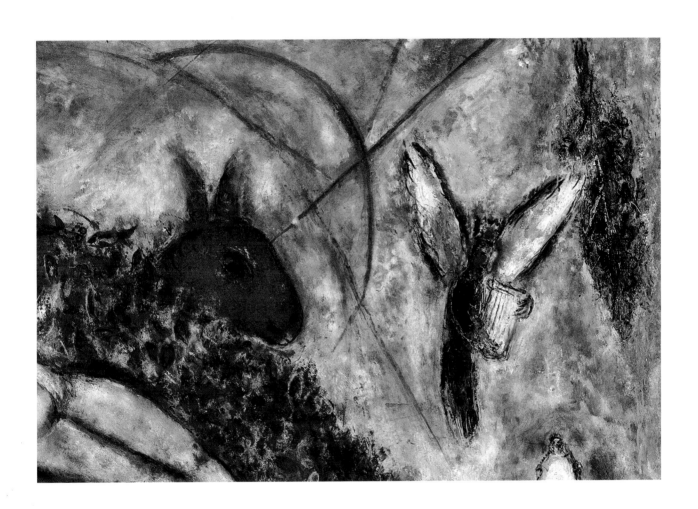

The Song of Songs III

1960

Oil on paper mounted

on canvas

H. 149; L. 210 cm.

This painting features a complex composition divided into sections by three arcs.

In the upper part of the painting, two circles clearly evoke a woman's breasts. Below, another curving line underscoring the first two seems to outline her abdomen.

Superimposed on the left circle, a couple stands beneath a kuppah, or wedding canopy, held up by two angels. The bride and groom, whose bodies merge, resemble shooting stars. An angel carries a lighted candelabra with three branches, while another angel blows into a *shofar*. A group of people at the couple's feet – the wedding party – is celebrating the joyous event. A dove, the symbol of peace, is hovering above the angel musician.

A central motif appears: two mirror-image cities reflecting each other on either side of a randomly-drawn line. Vence can be recognized by its ramparts and cathedral, and Vitebsk, upside-down, by its Orthodox church and little houses. In the sky of Vitebsk, a Jew with a knapsack on his back symbolizes the painter, who left Russia for Paris and, after a long, circuitous journey, eventually arrived in Vence.

As if to dispel any doubts that he sought to depict his world this picture, Chagall painted a self-portrait with his palette and brushes.

In the lower part of the painting, the newlyweds lying down might represent Chagall and his first wife, Bella. The bride's eyes are closed. Although King David is not depicted in this work, the presence of a crowned ass, a messianic symbol, recalls the cycle's theme.

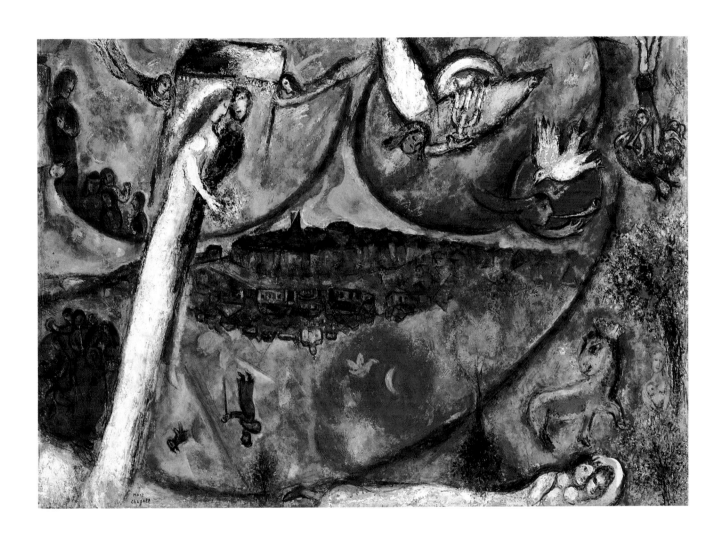

The Song of Songs IV

1958

Oil on paper mounted
on canvas

H. 144.5; L. 210.5 cm.

A diagonally-pitched, winged horse surrounded by dark red tones carries a couple locked in an embrace who can be identified as David and Bathsheba. Pegasus, the winged horse of Greek mythology, symbolizes poetry. In his front hooves he is holding a bouquet as an offering. The couple riding the horse is depicted as a comet. The mythological creature does not have hind legs; the bride's gown is floating.

The presence of the flying horse also the evokes the power of desire and sexual love.

Above, the city of Jerusalem can be recognized by the Tower of David. The atmosphere is incandescent. All the characters in the *Biblical Message* appear in the lower part of the painting: wandering Jews, women carrying children, rabbis and lovers. David's face is green, as though Chagall painted him to illustrate the Yiddish saying, "green with emotion."

The Song of Songs V

1965-1966

Oil on paper mounted

on canvas

H. 150; L. 226 cm.

The last painting in the Song of Songs cycle sums up the series in this room.

A multicolored sun shines on a couple, King David, a naked woman, the cities in Chagall's life and music.

Unlike the revolving sun in the Creation painting, this aster has star-shaped rays. The composition features two cities that were close to Chagall's heart separated by the bridge spanning the Dvina in Vitebsk, the town where the painter was born, which can be recognized on the hill on the right. Jerusalem is on the left, and to let there be no mistake, Chagall painted David's throne with the two lions of the tribe of Judah and the word "Jerusalem" written in Hebrew.

David, the psalm-writing king, floats towards his bride in the sky above the city. The sovereign's head is partly hidden by a bird, but his profile can be made out. At his feet, an ass, the animal that symbolizes messianism, is wearing the crown which is the attribute of David's royalty. Indeed, David was considered the Messiah. The diaphanous bride looks like a phantom or an evanescent dream.

This painting, which is the high point of the Song of Songs series, features all the themes that Chagall developed in the four previous works.

The Donated Works

In 1973 the Musée national Message Biblique Marc Chagall opened thanks to the generosity of Marc and Valentina Chagall and the painter's friendship with André Malraux, who originally had the idea for the project.

When Marc Chagall died in 1985, his heirs gave 46 paintings and 379 works on paper to the French government in lieu of inheritance taxes. The Musée national d'art moderne stored ten paintings from that group at the Musée national Message Biblique.

The triptych *Resistance, Resurrection, Liberation* was at the origin of a major composition that Chagall entitled *Revolution.* The artist completed the initial work in 1937 for the twentieth anniversary of the Russian Revolution. In 1943, Chagall divided the painting into three parts, which he reworked separately until 1953.

In the 1950s, the artist focused on Biblical themes. Chagall had already painted scenes from the Old and New Testaments twenty years earlier, and now he was to add the *Biblical Message* series. During the same period, he painted other versions of *Moses Receiving the Tables of the Law, The Crossing of the Red Sea* and, lastly, *King David.*

He also depicted Old and New Testament scenes, including *The Prophet Jeremiah, Passover* and *Easter* and the *Descent from the Cross.* In *Exodus,* Chagall mixed references to contemporary life with Bible scenes.

Resistance

1937-1948

Oil on canvas

H. 168; L. 103 cm.

Resurrection

1937-1948

Oil on canvas

H. 168.3; L. 107.7 cm.

Liberation

1937-1952

Oil on canvas

H. 168; L. 88 cm.

Moses receiving the Tables of the Law

1950-1952

Oil on canvas

H. 194.5; L. 129.8 cm.

King David

1951

Oil on canvas

H. 198; L. 133 cm.

The Exodus

1952-1966

Oil on canvas

H. 130; L. 162.3 cm.

The Parting of the Red sea

1955

Oil on canvas

H. 216.5; L. 146 cm.

The Prophet Jeremiah

1968

Oil on canvas

H. 115; L. 146.3 cm.

Passover and Easter

1968

Oil on canvas

H. 160.3; L. 159.3 cm.

The Descent from the Cross

1968-1976

Oil on canvas

H. 150; L. 188 cm.

Monumental Works

Tapestry

1971

Woven at the Gobelins work-

shop by Evelyne Lelong

H. 226; L. 322 cm.

The tapestry was woven by the heddle-setter Evelyne Lelong at the Gobelins workshop in Paris. It features two cities that were close to Chagall's heart.

The walled town of Vence, where Chagall lived, is shown in brown tones. The blue sea is in the middle of the tapestry, and the white city of Jerusalem is on the right. A sun shines above the cities. A man is reading a book beneath a tree.

Another sun, a fish, a bird and horse – perhaps an evocation of the four elements – are above Vence. A double portrait floats in the air; the two faces have merged into one.

Mosaic: *The Prophet Elijah*

1970

Mosaic made by Lino Melano

H. 715; L. 570 cm.

A small, temporary exhibition room is illuminated by a large bay window overlooking a pool. The water reflects a wall mosaic depicting the wheel of the zodiac with the prophet Elijah on his chariot of fire in the center.

Elijah is standing and lifting his arms. The chariot, pulled by three horses, seems to rise heavenward. Above, there is a crescent moon. The twelve signs of the zodiac are around the prophet.

This motif recalls ancient pavement mosaics in which the signs of the zodiac are also arranged around a central figure driving a chariot: Helios, the personification of the sun.

Chagall departed from classical tradition by not depicting the four seasons in the corners of the mosaic, and Elijah's chariot is pulled by three horses instead of the quadriga driven by Helios.

A crescent moon is above the prophet, but Elijah ascended in broad daylight instead of at night. By setting the scene in the daytime, Chagall wanted to demarcate the difference between the mythological and the religious.

The mosaic's background is a landscape. The sea and the buildings in the upper part of the work suggest the environs of Nice. Trees are in the lower part. One of them is lying down just below the sign of Libra. Bella, whom Chagall called his tree of life, passed away in September 1944.

The Stained Glass Windows: *The Creation of the World*

In the late 1960s, when the decision to build the Marc Chagall Biblical Message Museum was made, the artist wanted a concert hall that would also be a place where visitors could come to rest and meditate. To finalize this project he called upon the master glass craftsman Charles Marq, with whom he made almost all the windows.

Remaining faithful to the theme of the *Biblical Message*, Chagall chose to depict the creation of the world.

He illustrated the seven days of the Creation in three windows that decrease in size from right to left.

The first and largest window, which begins the cycle on the right-hand side, shows the first four days, when God divided heaven from earth, created day and night and separated "the waters which were under the firmament from the waters which were above the firmament". From the water "under the firmament" He separated dry land, on which He sowed the seeds that brought forth grass and trees. And on the fourth day, God created the stars and the sun to "give light upon the earth".

Chagall used dark blue to symbolize the Creation. Geometrical forms of various colors – yellow for the sun and stars, green for the grass, brown for the earth – are distributed around the long diagonal lines which seem to unite God with his handiwork.

The smaller, middle window illustrates the fifth and sixth days, when God created the fish, the birds, wild beasts "after their kind" and, lastly, man and woman in his image.

This stained glass window takes up the themes of the *Biblical Message*: the tempting serpent, and the Tree of Knowledge under which Adam and Eve hold each other in an embrace. Animals – a goat, fish and bird – seem to be floating in the air.

The last stained glass window, and the narrowest of the three, depicts the day God rested. Chagall used an angel to symbolize the Sabbath. Motionless geometric shapes divide the surface of the window. The world is stabilized, finished, and there is no need for motifs in motion.

These stained glass windows provide the room with an atmosphere of serenity that was sought by Chagall. Their theme and arrangement from right to left, the direction in which Hebrew is read, give them an almost sacred character.

The auditorium

Biography

1887

Marc Chagall is born in Vitebsk, a small town in present-day Belarus, on July 7, 1887.

1906

Chagall enters Yehuda Penn's painting studio in Vitebsk.

1907-1909

Lives in Saint Petersburg, where he works in Leon Bakst's studio.

1910

The patron Maxim Vinaver offers him a grant to study in Paris.

1911-1912

Chagall moves into one of the studios at La Ruche, where many artists already live. There he meets Robert and Sonia Delaunay, André Salmon and Chaïm Soutine, and becomes friends with Blaise Cendrars. His earliest works: *To Russia, To Asses and to Others, The Holy Carter, Me and the Village, Homage to Apollinaire* are acclaimed by Guillaume Apollinaire.

1913-1914

Exhibits the paintings *Birth, Adam and Eve, The Fiddler* and *Self-Portrait with Seven Fingers* at the Salon des Indépendants. In July 1914, he exhibits at the Der Sturm gallery in Berlin.

1914-1915

Chagall returns to Vitebsk. The First World War breaks out. He marries Bella Rosenfeld.

1916-1918

His daughter, Ida, is born. Chagall produces many paintings. Lives in Moscow. Exhibits at Le Valet de carreau. He is appointed to the position of fine arts commissar for Vitebsk and director of the city's school of fine arts.

1919

Artistic differences between Chagall and Malevich at the Vitebsk academy of fine arts.

1920

In May, Chagall leaves Vitebsk for Moscow.

1920-1923

Chagall draws up plans and creates models for Moscow's Jewish Kammeny Theater, for which he paints murals entitled *Introduction to Jewish Theater, Theater, Dance, Music* and *The Wedding Table*. In 1922, he leaves Moscow for Berlin.

1925

First engravings in Berlin for Paul Cassirer illustrating his autobiographical text, *My Life*. Leaves Berlin for Paris.

1924-1925

Moves to 101 rue d'Orléans and revives his friendship with Sonia and Robert Delaunay. Meets André Malraux for the first time. The art dealer Ambroise Vollard commissions him to illustrate Gogol's *Dead Souls*.

1926

Illustrates La Fontaine's *Fables* on Vollard's request. First exhibition in New York.

1927-1930

Stays in various parts of France. Vollard commissions him to illustrate the Bible.

1931

Travels to Palestine. Paints preparatory gouaches for his Bible engravings.

1932-1936

Many trips to the Netherlands, Italy and England. First major retrospective at the Basel museum. Travels to Spain and Poland.

1937

Chagall takes out French citizenship.

1938

Exhibition at the Palais des Beaux-Arts in Brussels.

1939

Chagall wins the Carnegie Foundation Prize. At the outbreak of war, he takes refuge in Gordes, in Provence.

1941

The persecution of the Jews forces Chagall to leave Europe. In New York, he meets other refugee artists and writers, including Léger, Bernanos, Masson, Maritain, Mondrian and Breton.

1942-1944

Chagall designs the sets and costumes for Tchaikowsky's ballet *Aleko* and paints a series of works inspired by the war: *Obsession, The Yellow Crucifixion, War*.

1944

His wife, Bella, dies.

1945-1946

After one year of creative silence, Chagall begins painting again. He designs the sets and costumes for Stravinsky's *Firebird*. First color lithographs for *The Thousand and One Nights*.

1947

A series of retrospective exhibitions is held in Europe.

1948

Chagall returns definitively to France.

1949-1952

Moves to Vence, in Provence. Meets Valentina Brodsky, whom he marries on July 12, 1952. Chagall finds the happiness and balance he needs. A new and fruitful period of creation begins.

1953-1957

Many trips and exhibitions. Begins the *Biblical Message* series of paintings.

1958

Meets the stained-glass master craftsman Charles Marq; the two men work closely together in the future. Designs the sets and costumes for *Daphnis and Chloe*.

1959-1966
Chagall develops his Bible-based work. Designs stained-glass windows for the cathedral of Metz, the Hadassah center in Jerusalem and the United Nations in New York. French culture minister Malraux supports his work and commissions him to paint the ceiling of the Paris opera house. Chagall also paints two large murals for the Metropolitan Opera house in New York. Working with his friend Charles Sorlier, his lithograph output increases.

1966
Marc and Valentina Chagall leave Vence for Saint-Paul-de-Vence.

1967-1969
Marc and Valentina Chagall donate the seventeen large paintings in the Biblical Message series to the French government. Chagall continues his monumental work. Designs stained-glass windows, tapestries and mosaics, especially *Ulysees' Message* for the law and economics department at the University of Nice.

1969-1970
The "Homage à Marc Chagall" exhibition is held at the Grand Palais in Paris. Retrospective of prints at the Bibliothèque nationale in Paris. Stained-glass windows for the Fraumünster in Zurich. Under the impetus of André Malraux, the decision is made to build the Musée National du Message Biblique Marc Chagall in Nice.

1971-1973
Numerous exhibitions, most notably at the Tretiakov gallery in Moscow.

July 3, 1973
Inauguration of the Musée National du Message Biblique Marc Chagall in Nice, with André Malraux in attendance.

1974-1977
Chagall designs a monumental mosaic, *The Four Seasons*, for Chicago, stained-glass windows for Sarrebourg and Mainz and the mosaic for the Sainte Roseline chapel in Les Arcs (Var). French president Valérie Giscard d'Estaing awards him the Grand-Croix of the Legion of Honor.

1978-1981
Exhibition at the Pitti palace in Florence. Inauguration of the stained-glass windows in Chichester, England and at the Art Institute of Chicago. At the request of Aimé Maeght, Chagall produces fourteen very large lithographs that are among the finest engravings he ever made.

1984
Three major exhibitions celebrate Chagall's 97th birthday: at the Centre Georges Pompidou in Paris, the Maeght Foundation in Saint-Paul-de-Vence and the Musée National du Message Biblique Marc Chagall in Nice.

1985
Chagall's health declines, but he continues to work. He dies on March 26, 1985.

A publication of the publishing department directed by Béatrice Foulon

Editorial coordination:
Marie-Claude Bianchini

Art design and layout:
Cover:
Gilles Huot / H.D.L. Design

Interior:
Cécile Neuville

Preparation of the texts:
Annie Desvachez

Production:
Jacques Venelli

Photoengraving:
Bussière

Translation:
Glenn Naumovitz

Relecture:
Ann Cremin

Printed and bound in December 2000
by Kapp Lahure Jombart

Copyright registration: December 2000
ISBN: 2-7118-3939-7
GA 20 3939